STUD

PEOPLE IN THE WORLD

WILFREDO DE JESÚS

M000191168

WHAT HAPPENS WHEN
GOD'S PEOPLE STAND STRONG

IN THE GAP

Influence
RESOURCES

Published by Influence Resources
1445 N. Boonville Ave.
Springfield, Missouri 65802

www.InfluenceResources.com

Interior Design by Mellowtown.com

Copyright and use of template is retained
by Brett Eastman.

ISBN 978-1-62912-097-3

17 16 15 14 • 1 2 3 4

Printed in the United States of America

CONTENTS

INTRODUCTION

WELCOME TO IN THE GAP!

Welcome to a six-session study in which you will be inspired by the stories of some heroes and heroines of the faith, and grow in your own faith as well. Each of the individuals will either show us how to stand in the gap or share how others have stood in the gap for them. These people answer the challenge found in Ezekiel 22:30:

"I looked for someone among them who would build up the wall and stand before me in the gap on behalf of the land so I would not have to destroy it, but I found no one."

What is a gap? A gap is a place of weakness, vulnerability, and danger. It is a defenseless location of exposure and limitation, a point where people face real threats. Gaps exist in our countries, our communities, and at home with our families. And individually

Huge gaps have opened up in our world. Do we even notice? Do we care? God is asking, "Will you stand in the gap for these people? Will you stand in the gap for My sake and My glory?"

Who is the kind of person God is looking for, the type of man or woman, young or old, who has insight into the problem and courage to take bold action? God isn't looking for people who feel no fear. He's looking for people who walk toward their fear and stand in the gap to help those in need.

Will you choose to answer this call and stand in the gap for others?

WILFREDO DE JESÚS
Senior Pastor of New Life Covenant Church
Chicago, Illinois

HOW TO USE THIS
STUDY GUIDE

....

THIS STUDY GUIDE'S CONTENTS ARE IN TWO SECTIONS:

....

This study consists of six sessions, each focused on one biblical character who stood in the gap for their people, obeying God's call with faith. You'll have a chance to learn together, to discuss and share your own stories in a way that focuses on practical real-life application.

SESSIONS

In addition to the written study, this curriculum includes a DVD with teaching and testimonies. Author Wilfredo De Jesús (Pastor Choco) will introduce each session's theme. Then you will hear the stories of real people who share their testimonies about standing in the gap or those who stood in the gap for them. This is followed by a short teaching segment from Pastor Choco. We hope their stories inspire, instruct, and challenge you to grow in your relationship with God.

In your discussion, you'll dig into the Bible, but also respond to what you watched on the DVD. Use this book as a guide, not a straitjacket. If the group responds to the video in an unexpected, but honest way, go with that. If you think of a better question than the one shown, ask it. Our prayer is that you would experience God in a fresh way as a result of this study, and that your faith would grow in a way that amazes you.

EXTRA HELPS

Familiarize yourself with the various items included in this section following the sessions. You may wish to incorporate some of them into the sessions themselves. If you are facilitating/leading a small group, this section will give you advice from experienced leaders both to encourage you and to help you avoid many common obstacles to effective small group leadership.

OUTLINE OF
EACH SESSION

A TYPICAL GROUP SESSION FOR THE IN THE GAP STUDY WILL INCLUDE THE FOLLOWING:

THEME VERSE AND INTRODUCTION. Each session will open with a theme verse and a brief introduction based on Pastor Choco's insights from the *In the Gap* book. Make it a practice to read these before the session.

SHARE YOUR STORY. The foundation for spiritual growth is an intimate connection with God and His family. That connection is built by sharing your story with a few people who really know you and who earn your trust. This section includes some simple questions to get your group talking—letting you share as much or as little of your story as you want.

HEAR GOD'S STORY. with the DVD teaching segments. In this section, you'll watch the DVD segment featuring inspiring testimonies of modern-day people who are standing in the gap. Then you'll read from the Bible to hear God's story—and begin to see how your story aligns with His story. When the study directs you, you'll return to the DVD and watch a short teaching segment.

CHANGE YOUR STORY. God wants you to stand in the gap too. As you discover the gap areas in your own life, you'll have the opportunity to ask God to help you to stand, to pray, and to wait on Him.

DAILY DEVOTIONS. These pages provide Scriptures to read and reflect on between group meetings. This is a chance to slow down, to read just a small portion of Scripture each day, and to reflect and pray through it. Don't get in a hurry; take enough time to hear God's voice of love. Also take time to meditate on or memorize the theme verses for each session. We encourage you to give this important habit a try. The verses for the six sessions are listed on the inside front cover.

If you want to **STAND IN THE GAP** for **PEOPLE** in your **FAMILY** or your **COMMUNITY**, some people will ridicule you, mock you, and try to intimidate you. **YOUR COURAGE AND FAITH** threaten them, so they'll do anything they can to make you compromise.... But our task is to **CLING TENACIOUSLY TO CHRIST**, to trust Him for wisdom and strength, and to **STAND STRONG** against the temptation to compromise our ethics, the truth, and the vision God has given us.

—In the Gap

SESSION ONE

THEME VERSE: "They said to me, 'Those who survived the exile and are back in the province are in great trouble and disgrace. The wall of Jerusalem is broken down, and its gates have been burned with fire.' When I heard these things, I sat down and wept. For some days I mourned and fasted and prayed before the God of heaven" **Nehemiah 1:3–4.**

NEHEMIAH

IDENTIFIED A PROBLEM TO SOLVE.

What situation do you have a heart for, so much that you are willing to take action to correct it? Perhaps God has given you a heart for your city—to proclaim the gospel there. Perhaps it's a friend who has wandered from faith—and God is asking you to stand in the gap for them and intercede on their behalf—and even to confront them in love, to bring them back to the truth.

Nehemiah's tears, his righteous anger at the situation in Jerusalem, with its broken-down walls, moved him to take steps of great courage. He boldly responded to what God had revealed to him.

What situation are you weeping over? Are you willing to take action to change that situation?

That's what Nehemiah did. And it just might be what God is calling you to do.

READ *IN THE GAP*, CHAPTER 1.

OPEN WITH PRAYER.

SHARE YOUR STORY

What do you think it means to "stand in the gap" for someone?

Describe a time when someone stepped in and made a difference for you during a difficult time in your life.

Capture any key thoughts, questions,
and things you want to remember.

_____

_____

_____

_____

_____

_____

_____

_____

_____

_____

_____

_____

_____

_____

_____

_____

A Small Group Calendar (inside back cover) is a tool for planning who will host and lead
each meeting. Take a few minutes to plan hosts and leaders for your remaining meetings.
Don't pass this up! It will revolutionize your group.

DISCUSS THE FOLLOWING

We heard from a man who appreciated the other men who stepped into his life. One of those men redefined this man's image of believers. Who has made this kind of impact on your faith journey?

One man was homeless until an uncle stood in the gap for him. How can we stand in the gap for others in a tangible way?

One woman shared how a friend challenged her about a pattern of sin in her life. Have you ever done this? How do you confront someone, but not condemn them?

What can we learn from these individuals about standing in the gap?

When we read the true stories of Scripture, we learn what God is like. We see His plan unfolding, and we learn principles for our own lives.

As our first biblical example of someone who stood in the gap, Nehemiah demonstrates how a gap person identifies a problem to solve.

THE GAP IS A **PLACE OF WEAKNESS,** VULNERABILITY, AND DANGER— A PLACE OF **REAL** THREATS.

Capture any key thoughts, questions,
and things you want to remember.

_____

_____

_____

_____

_____

_____

_____

_____

DISCUSS THE FOLLOWING

**In the video, Pastor Choco said, "With revelation comes
responsibility." What was revealed to Nehemiah?**

What responsibility did he take on?

READ NEHEMIAH 1:1–11

If you were introducing Nehemiah to a close friend, how would you describe him?

What was Nehemiah's initial response when he heard about the problems in Jerusalem? What did he do? (See verse 4 and following verses.)

What did the ruined wall of Jerusalem represent to Nehemiah? Why was he so upset about it?

READ NEHEMIAH 2:1–10

Nehemiah prayed, and his prayer led to his plan. How did Nehemiah stand in the gap?

Pastor Choco reminded us that when we try to rebuild walls, we will meet challenges. What walls are you trying to rebuild, and what challenges have arisen in that process?

READ NEHEMIAH 4:7–18

How did Nehemiah handle the potential attack of his enemies?

What are ways we can prepare for the attacks we face as we stand in the gap?

CHANGE YOUR STORY

GOD WANTS US TO BE A PART OF HIS KINGDOM—TO WEAVE OUR STORY INTO HIS. BY SMALL, SIMPLE CHOICES, WE BEGIN TO CHANGE OUR DIRECTION. THE HOLY SPIRIT HELPS US ALONG THE WAY TO IDENTIFY THE GAPS IN OUR LIVES AND THEN GIVES US THE STRENGTH TO STAND IN THEM.

Nehemiah understood a profound truth: If you're experiencing a great difficulty, and you're ready to undertake a great work, then you need the power of a great God. How can you apply this wisdom to your life as you stand in the gap?

PERSONAL
REFLECTION

Nehemiah shows us the importance of identifying the problem to solve. Where is God asking you to step out in faith to stand in the gap and begin to repair something that is broken?

PRAYING
TOGETHER

Look at Nehemiah's prayer in Nehemiah 1:5–11.
He begins with praise, then confession, and ends with his requests. Find each of these elements in the text. How can we use
this prayer as a model for our own prayers about gap situations in
our lives?

How can the group pray for you? (Add others' prayer requests
here.)

CLOSE IN PRAYER.

DAILY
DEVOTIONS

....

"THEY SAID TO ME, 'THOSE WHO SURVIVED THE EXILE AND
ARE BACK IN THE PROVINCE ARE IN GREAT TROUBLE AND
DISGRACE. THE WALL OF JERUSALEM IS BROKEN DOWN, AND
ITS GATES HAVE BEEN BURNED WITH FIRE.' WHEN I HEARD
THESE THINGS, I SAT DOWN AND WEPT. FOR SOME DAYS I
MOURNED AND FASTED AND PRAYED BEFORE THE GOD OF
HEAVEN" NEHEMIAH 1:3-4.

Developing our ability to follow the leading of the Holy Spirit takes
time and persistence. Learning how to stand in the gap comes to us
day-by-day as we:

PRAY. Commit to personal prayer and daily connection with God.
(You may find it helpful to write your prayers in a journal.)
Remember to pray for the requests shared by your fellow group
members.

MEMORIZE. Reflect on what God is saying about standing in the gap
for others by learning a passage of Scripture like the Theme Verse
above.

DAILY DEVOTIONS. Complete the Daily Devotions section. Each day, you'll
read just one portion of a passage of Scripture. Give prayerful
consideration to what God is telling you. Take your time! Ponder
and reflect. Then record your thoughts, insights, or prayer in the
Reflect section below the verses you read. On the sixth day, record
a summary of what you have learned about standing in the gap
through this study.

DAILY DEVOTIONS

Day 1.

NEHEMIAH 1:5
"Lord, the God of heaven, the great and awesome God, who keeps his covenant of love with those who love him and keep his commandments."

REFLECT:
Nehemiah begins his prayer by acknowledging God's power and reminding Him of His covenant with Israel. Why is it important to begin our prayers with a focus on God's goodness?

Day 2.

NEHEMIAH 1:6-7
"Let your ear be attentive and your eyes open to hear the prayer your servant is praying before you day and night for your servants, the people of Israel. I confess the sins we Israelites, including myself and my father's family, have committed against you. We have acted very wickedly toward you. We have not obeyed the commands, decrees and laws you gave your servant Moses."

REFLECT:
Why is confession important when we are asking God to help us fix what is broken?

Day 3.

NEHEMIAH 1:8-9
"Remember the instruction you gave your servant Moses, saying, 'If you are unfaithful, I will scatter you among the nations, but if you return to me and obey my commands, then even if your exiled people are at the farthest horizon, I will gather them from there and bring them to the place I have chosen as a dwelling for my Name.'"

REFLECT:
Nehemiah reminds God (and himself) of God's promises. What promises do you need to review? Where are you feeling discouraged and abandoned, as Israel was at this time?

Day 4.

NEHEMIAH 1:10
"They are your servants and your people, whom you redeemed by your great strength and your mighty hand."

REFLECT:
Nehemiah again prays in a way that lifts God up, that honors Him and praises His strength, and acknowledges that He is greater than we are—we are His servants.

Day 5.

NEHEMIAH 1:11
"Lord, let your ear be attentive to the prayer of this your servant and to the prayer of your servants who delight in revering your name. Give your servant success today by granting him favor in the presence of this man."

REFLECT:
What does Nehemiah ask for as he finally gets to the part of his prayer where he offers up requests?

Day 6.

SUMMARY
Use the following space to write any thoughts God has put in your heart and mind about how and where you need to stand in the gap for yourself and others.

TAKING ACTION
How will you put these insights into action?

SESSION TWO

THEME VERSE: "Do not think that because you are in the king's house you alone of all the Jews will escape. For if you remain silent at this time, relief and deliverance for the Jews will arise from another place, but you and your father's family will perish. And who knows but that you have come to your royal position for such a time as this?" **Esther 4:13–14.**

ESTHER
UNDERSTOOD HER TIMES.

magine being a young woman, possibly even a teenager, living as a foreigner in an unfriendly country. Now imagine being brought into the palace of the king—without having a say in the matter. Esther could have thought of herself as a victim.

Then Esther was chosen to be queen of the land. She went from having almost nothing to having everything to lose. But God asked her to see herself as a heroine—someone who could use her unusual circumstances to stand in the gap for others—to see herself as powerful, not powerless.

Might God be asking you to do the same—to be a voice for the voiceless? To step up to help others who need you? Who is He asking you to stand in the gap for, like Esther, with courage that says, "If I perish, I perish"?

READ *IN THE GAP,* CHAPTER 2.

OPEN WITH PRAYER.

SHARE YOUR STORY

Looking back at the last session about Nehemiah, what is one idea that stuck with you? How has it impacted you?

Today, we are talking about Esther. Have you ever found yourself in a situation you didn't expect to be in, where you had to "step up" and be courageous? What happened?

Capture any key thoughts, questions,
and things you want to remember.

DISCUSS THE FOLLOWING

Which of the individuals' testimonies was most meaningful to you? What made it stand out to you?

Like Esther and her cousin, Mordecai, one of the men described standing in the gap for his younger sister. What was his desire for his sister's life?

What can we learn from these individuals about standing in the gap for others?

HEAR GOD'S STORY

How can we become a part of God's story? By aligning our stories with His. As a biblical example, Esther shows us how to be a voice for the voiceless, even if it means risking everything.

Capture any key thoughts, questions,
and things you want to remember.

DISCUSS THE FOLLOWING

In the video, Pastor Choco said the Book of Esther is unusual
because God is not mentioned by name, but His providence is
evident in Esther's story. Why do you think God opted to remain
nameless in this book?

READ ESTHER 4:7–17

What threat are the Jews facing in this story?

Esther is challenged to step up and stand in the gap for her people. What is her first response?

What does Esther risk by going to talk to the king? What does Mordecai reminder her she's risking if she doesn't go to talk to the king?

In this passage, we see a shift in Esther—instead of just taking direction from Mordecai, she steps into a leadership role and tells him what to do. What do you think caused this shift ?

READ ESTHER 7:1–6

At a banquet with the king and Haman, enemy of the Jews, how did Esther stand in the gap for her people?

In *In the Gap*, Pastor Choco says, "God didn't use someone who had a great background, had lived a pure life, and always faithfully obeyed Him. God used someone who was deeply flawed, had divided priorities, and was not even aware of the problem until someone told her about it.

How can Esther's example inspire us?

CHANGE YOUR STORY

GOD WANTS US TO BE PART OF HIS KINGDOM—TO WEAVE OUR STORY INTO HIS. THE HOLY SPIRIT HELPS US TO IDENTIFY THE GAPS IN OTHERS' LIVES AND THEN GIVES US THE STRENGTH TO STAND IN THOSE GAPS.

Esther understood her times. When her people faced death, Esther could have opted to ignore the situation or sit back and wait for the events to unfold. But she didn't. Tell the group about a time someone challenged you to step into the gap when you didn't want to—in a similar way to Esther. What happened?

PERSONAL
REFLECTION

In his book, Pastor Choco reminds us that like Esther we might be at a crossroads between someone's desperate need and God's desire to use us. But people make excuses, blame others for not taking action, or even minimize or deny that the problem exists. What keeps you from standing in the gap for others?

PRAYING
TOGETHER

Look at Esther's direction for the Jews in Esther 4:15–16. Why did Esther ask Mordecai to tell all the Jews in the city to fast?

Together through fasting and prayer, they saw God overcome an impossible situation. How can the group pray together for you? (Add others' prayer requests here.)

CLOSE IN PRAYER.

DAILY
DEVOTIONS

"DO NOT THINK THAT BECAUSE YOU ARE IN THE KING'S HOUSE YOU ALONE OF ALL THE JEWS WILL ESCAPE. FOR IF YOU REMAIN SILENT AT THIS TIME, RELIEF AND DELIVERANCE FOR THE JEWS WILL ARISE FROM ANOTHER PLACE, BUT YOU AND YOUR FATHER'S FAMILY WILL PERISH. AND WHO KNOWS BUT THAT YOU HAVE COME TO YOUR ROYAL POSITION FOR SUCH A TIME AS THIS?" **ESTHER 4:13-14.**

Developing our ability to follow the leading of the Holy Spirit takes time and persistence. Learning how to stand in the gap comes to us day-by-day as we:

PRAY. Commit to personal prayer and daily connection with God. (You may find it helpful to write your prayers in a journal.) Remember to pray for the requests shared by your fellow group members.

MEMORIZE. Reflect on what God is saying about standing in the gap for others by learning a passage of Scripture like the Theme Verse above.

DAILY DEVOTIONS. Complete the Daily Devotions section. Each day, you'll read just one portion of a passage of Scripture. Give prayerful consideration to what God is telling you. Take your time! Ponder and reflect. Then record your thoughts, insights, or prayer in the Reflect section below the verses you read. On the sixth day, record a summary of what you have learned about standing in the gap through this study.

DAILY
DEVOTIONS

Day 1.

PSALM 18:25–26
"To the faithful you show yourself faithful, to the blameless you show yourself blameless, to the pure you show yourself pure, but to the devious you show yourself shrewd."

REFLECT:
What attributes of God does this passage call us to imitate? What promises does it make to us about God?

Day 2.

PSALM 18:27
"You save the humble but bring low those whose eyes are haughty."

REFLECT:
How can we be humble and yet strong at the same time? How does God's saving us strengthen us?

Day 3.

PSALM 18:28
"You, Lord, keep my lamp burning; my God turns my darkness into light."

REFLECT:
This verse uses a metaphor of light and a lamp. What do you think this symbolizes? What does it mean that God keeps our lamp burning?

Day 4.

PSALM 18:29

"With your help I can advance against a troop; with my God I can scale a wall."

REFLECT:

What impossible task do you need God's help with right now? What battle do you need Him to fight on your behalf?

Day 5.

PSALM 18:30

"As for God, his way is perfect: The Lord's word is flawless; he shields all who take refuge in him."

REFLECT:

What promise does this verse make to us. How can we find that "refuge" this verse talks about? (Hint: Look at the beginning of the verse.)

Day 6.

SUMMARY

Use the following space to write any thoughts God has put in your heart and mind about standing in the gap for others.

TAKING ACTION

How will you put these insights into action?

SESSION THREE

THEME VERSE: "Noah did everything just as God commanded him" **Genesis 6:22.**

NOAH

WAS ALL IN, NO MATTER WHAT THE COST.

Imagine you've heard an unmistakable message from God. It requires radical obedience and risk. Confirmation that you've heard God correctly and done the right thing comes . . . 120 years later!

Would you stay faithful? Would you keep going, obeying, doing what God had told you to do? Would you ignore the ridicule of others, the doubts in your own mind?

That's what happened to Noah. But Noah was all in, no matter what the cost. He stood in the gap for a wicked generation, offering them a chance to repent and receive God's grace. They all turned him down, mocking his ideas and his actions: building an ark in the

desert, preparing for a flood that they were sure would never happen.

The people had no idea what danger they were in. And it may be that you are standing in the gap for someone—maybe a family member or friend. They have no idea the calamity that is just around the corner in their life—but you can see it coming. The fallout from addiction, moral compromise, habitual sin—it's coming. You're praying for them, hoping they'll turn around before they hit the wall.

Like Noah, are you willing to be all in, even when you face ridicule or feel like the only one who is obeying God? Who knows? Maybe you'll be a blessing to future generations, just as Noah was.

READ *IN THE GAP*, CHAPTER 3.

When a society experiences moral failure. God looks for a man or a woman to stand in the gap—someone who will have hope when everything seems hopeless. to have faith when the situation is dark and dire. and to lead when almost no one will follow. God found Noah.
—*In the Gap*, **Wilfredo De Jesús**

Standing *IN THE GAP* for people can **BE INSPIRING** to others. Telling our PERSONAL STORIES builds deeper **CONNECTIONS** among group members. USE THIS TIME to SHARE YOUR STORY of God at work through **YOUR LIFE**.

OPEN WITH PRAYER.

Have you, or someone you know, ever received what seemed like a strange assignment from God? What happened?

Tell about a time you had to make a commitment to be all in on a mission, a project, or a risky venture. What happened?

Capture any key thoughts, questions,
and things you want to remember.

DISCUSS THE FOLLOWING

Each individual shared about standing in the gap:

- Pastor Choco has invested his life in the community he grew up in.
- A young woman, who had turned away from God, had a friend who declared she wouldn't let her friend die on her watch.
- A man shared how friends have been faithful support during his child's illness.
- One man's wife convinced him that he needed to get his life straight in order to be there for his daughters.

What do these individuals teach us about standing in the gap?

HEAR GOD'S STORY

WHEN WE READ THE TRUE STORIES OF SCRIPTURE, WE LEARN WHAT GOD IS LIKE. WE SEE HIS PLAN UNFOLDING, AND WE LEARN PRINCIPLES FOR OUR OWN LIVES.

Noah stood in the gap in righteousness even though people ridiculed him. He shows us how to be godly in a godless generation.

Capture any key thoughts, questions,
and things you want to remember.

_____

_____

_____

_____

_____

_____

_____

_____

_____

DISCUSS THE FOLLOWING

What three arks are mentioned in the Bible? What is the significance of each one?

Pastor Choco told his own story of people laughing at him for doing what God asked him to do. How can his story encourage us?

READ GENESIS 6:5–22

In what ways is the culture of Noah's day similar to our own? In what ways is it different?

Imagine yourself in the story as one of Noah's sons or daughters-in-law. What are you thinking and feeling when you first hear Noah's plan? How do you feel when you get recruited to help build the ark? How do you feel when you're on board and the rain is falling?

READ JAMES 1:2–8

Noah was faithful during 120 years of hard work. What promise does this passage give us to help us be faithful?

What do you think it means to be "double-minded"? How does it keep us from being all in with our faith?

CHANGE YOUR STORY

GOD WANTS US TO BE PART OF HIS KINGDOM—TO WEAVE OUR STORY INTO HIS. THAT WILL MEAN CHANGE—TO GO HIS WAY RATHER THAN OUR OWN. THE HOLY SPIRIT HELPS US ALONG THE WAY, CHALLENGING US TO LOVE NOT ONLY THOSE AROUND US BUT THOSE FAR FROM GOD.

Noah shows us that we can expect opposition, ridicule, and mocking from others—even those we thought would support us and appreciate our efforts. Noah had no idea how much he would have to sacrifice when he said yes to God. It didn't matter. He was all in. Where is God asking you to be all in like Noah?

PERSONAL
REFLECTION

CHARACTER IS WHO WE ARE WHEN NO ONE IS LOOKING. REPUTATION IS PEOPLE'S PERCEPTION OF OUR CHARACTER. GOD IS FAR MORE CONCERNED ABOUT OUR CHARACTER THAN OUR REPUTATION. IF WE'RE SMART, WE'LL HAVE THE SAME PRIORITY.

What is one thing you need to change in order to be more like Noah, who walked faithfully with God?

PRAYING
TOGETHER

In the video, we heard that disbelief says, "I don't want to believe; I'm content in the darkness," while doubt says, "I want to see the light." Where are you struggling with doubt right now about God's purposes? Share, then pray for each other.

How can the group pray for you? (Add others' prayer requests here.)

CLOSE IN PRAYER.

DAILY
DEVOTIONS

"NOAH DID EVERYTHING JUST AS GOD COMMANDED HIM"
GENESIS 6:22.

Developing our ability to follow the leading of the Holy Spirit takes time and persistence. Learning how to stand in the gap comes to us day-by-day as we:

PRAY. Commit to personal prayer and daily connection with God. (You may find it helpful to write your prayers in a journal.) Remember to pray for the requests shared by your fellow group members.

MEMORIZE. Reflect on what God is saying about standing in the gap for others by learning a passage of Scripture like the Theme Verse above.

DAILY DEVOTIONS. Complete the Daily Devotions section. Each day, you'll read just one portion of a passage of Scripture. Give prayerful consideration to what God is telling you. Take your time! Ponder and reflect. Then record your thoughts, insights, or prayer in the Reflect section below the verses you read. On the sixth day, record a summary of what you have learned about standing in the gap through this study.

DAILY
DEVOTIONS

Day 1.

PSALM 34:4

"I sought the LORD, and he answered me; he delivered me from all my fears."

REFLECT:

What fears are threatening to flood your life right now? Ask God to deliver you.

Day 2.

PSALM 34:5

"Those who look to him are radiant; their faces are never covered with shame."

REFLECT:

Where do you wrestle with shame or feel inadequate? What does this verse tell us we can do to get free from shame?

Day 3.

PSALM 34:6

"This poor man called, and the LORD heard him; he saved him out of all his troubles."

REFLECT:

What promises do we find in this verse? What troubles are you facing that you need God to rescue you from?

Day 4.

PSALM 34:7
"The angel of the LORD encamps around those who fear him, and he delivers them."

REFLECT:
What does this verse tell us about God's protection of those He loves?

Day 5.

PSALM 34:8
"Taste and see that the LORD is good; blessed is the one who takes refuge in him."

REFLECT:
How can you "taste" God? How can you take refuge in Him? What's one step you can take to trust Him more?

Day 6.

SUMMARY
Use the following space to write any thoughts God has put in your heart and mind about standing in the gap for others.

TAKING ACTION
How will you put these insights into action?

SESSION FOUR

THEME VERSE: "Your servant has killed both the lion and the bear; this uncircumcised Philistine will be like one of them, because he has defied the armies of the living God. The LORD who rescued me from the paw of the lion and the paw of the bear will rescue me from the hand of this Philistine" **1 Samuel 17:36-37.**

DAVID

WAS ANOINTED BY GOD TO DO THE WORK.

There are times when life feels like a battle. We feel attacked, vulnerable—struggling against things too big for us to handle on our own. The truth is, we can't handle them on our own. We need God's help; and God wants to help us. If we are faithful and obedient to Him, we will be amazed at the strength and power that He gives us to fight even the strongest enemies.

We can be confident in knowing that as God equips, and as others stand in the gap for us, we will have victory over the difficulties in our lives. Where are you trusting God for a victory?

READ *IN THE GAP,* CHAPTER 4.

OPEN WITH PRAYER.

The Bible is full of stories of warriors for God. What do you think it means to be a warrior for God today?

SHARE YOUR STORY

IN THIS SESSION, WE ARE TALKING ABOUT DAVID. HE WENT FROM BEING A NOBODY—OVERLOOKED, DESPISED, AND FORSAKEN—UNTIL HE STOOD UP TO GOLIATH.

Where in your life it does feel like you are being attacked?

Capture any key thoughts, questions, and things you want to remember.

_____

_____

_____

_____

_____

_____

_____

_____

DISCUSS THE FOLLOWING

A couple shared how people helped them during a difficult time. What did people do to help them?

A pastor decided to stand in the gap in his community. What is one need in your community that your church could stand in the gap for?

HEAR GOD'S STORY

How can we become a part of God's story? By aligning our stories with His.

As a biblical example, David shows us that social activism needs to be more than a hobby for believers.

WILFREDO
DE JESÚS

IN
THE
GAP

WHAT HAPPENS WHEN
GOD'S PEOPLE STAND STRONG

Capture any key thoughts, questions,
and things you want to remember.

_____
_____
_____
_____
_____
_____
_____
_____
_____
_____
_____

DISCUSS THE FOLLOWING

**Pastor Choco asked, "Who is the giant God is asking you to fight?"
How would you answer this question in your life?**

READ 1 SAMUEL 17

How did Goliath taunt the Israelite soldiers?

David arrives on the scene and offers to fight the giant. What dis-
advantages did David have going into this battle? What strengths
did he have?

In the video, Pastor Choco talked about how David's "private"
experiences as a shepherd fighting off a lion and a bear prepared
him for his public battle with Goliath. What experiences is God
giving you right now that might be shaping you as preparation for
more public experiences to come?

In verse 47, David proclaimed: "All those gathered here will know
that it is not by sword or spear that the LORD saves; for the battle is the LORD's, and he will give all of you into our hands." For
most of us, we don't engage in combat with sword or spear. What
does the Lord give us to use in battle?

CHANGE YOUR STORY

GOD WANTS US TO BE PART OF HIS KINGDOM—TO WEAVE OUR STORY INTO HIS. THE HOLY SPIRIT HELPS US TO IDENTIFY THE GAPS IN OTHERS' LIVES AND THEN GIVES US THE STRENGTH TO STAND IN THOSE GAPS.

David was anointed by God to do the work. He demonstrated how to get involved in the big issues of our times for the right reasons—because we represent the King and His purposes on earth. Describe how someone has impressed you by standing publicly for what is right.

PERSONAL
REFLECTION

Pastor Choco talked about private preparation for public battles. What spiritual practices do you need to add to your life so that you will be prepared for future battles?

READ EPHESIANS 6:10-20

David knew exactly what weapons he needed to beat Goliath. Make a list of the various pieces of armor listed in this passage. Then write down or share how each would help you as you face the giants in your life.

PRAYING
TOGETHER

In the video, Pastor Choco reminded us that standing in the gap means to be vulnerable, to take a risk. How is God calling you to stand in the gap?

How can the group pray together for you? (Add others' prayer requests here.)

CLOSE IN PRAYER.

DAILY
DEVOTIONS

"YOUR SERVANT HAS KILLED BOTH THE LION AND THE BEAR; THIS UNCIRCUMCISED PHILISTINE WILL BE LIKE ONE OF THEM, BECAUSE HE HAS DEFIED THE ARMIES OF THE LIVING GOD. THE LORD WHO RESCUED ME FROM THE PAW OF THE LION AND THE PAW OF THE BEAR WILL RESCUE ME FROM THE HAND OF THIS PHILISTINE" 1 SAMUEL 17:36–37.

Developing our ability to follow the leading of the Holy Spirit takes time and persistence. Learning how to stand in gap comes to us day-by-day as we:

PRAY. Commit to personal prayer and daily connection with God. (You may find it helpful to write your prayers in a journal.) Remember to pray for the requests shared by your fellow group members.

MEMORIZE. Reflect on what God is saying about standing in the gap for others by learning a passage of Scripture like the Theme Verse above.

DAILY DEVOTIONS. Complete the Daily Devotions section. Each day, you'll read just one portion of a passage of Scripture. This Psalm was believed to have been written by David right after he defeated Goliath. Give prayerful consideration to what God is telling you. Take your time! Ponder and reflect. Then record your thoughts, insights, or prayer in the Reflect section below the verses you read. On the sixth day, record a summary of what you have learned about standing in the gap through this study.

DAILY
DEVOTIONS

Day 1.

PSALM 28:6
"Praise be to the LORD, for he has heard my cry for mercy."

REFLECT:
What are you crying out to God for right now, seeking HIs mercy?

Day 2.

PSALM 28:7
"The LORD is my strength and my shield; my heart trusts in him, and he helps me."

REFLECT:
Like David in battle, God promises to strengthen and shield us. Talk to Him about where you need strength, then affirm your trust in Him.

Day 3.

PSALM 28:7
"My heart leaps for joy, and with my song I praise him."

REFLECT:
What is something you can praise God for right now, even if you are in the midst of struggle? Write down one or two things you're grateful for. What happens to your heart?

Day 4.

PSALM 28:8
"The LORD is the strength of his people, a fortress of salvation for his anointed one."

REFLECT:
In what ways has God been a strong fortress for you recently? Spend some time just thanking Him for that.

have the Group Share Then ask one person To pray a prayer of Thanksgiving for Gods' strength

Day 5.

PSALM 28:9
"Save your people and bless your inheritance; be their shepherd and carry them forever."

REFLECT:
What does it mean to have God as your Shepherd? Why do you think this metaphor was significant to David? What does it mean to you?

Day 6.

SUMMARY
Use the following space to write any thoughts God has put in your heart and mind about standing in the gap for others.

TAKING ACTION
How will you put these insights into action?

SESSION FIVE

THEME VERSE: "Therefore encourage one another and build each other up, just as in fact you are doing" **1 Thessalonians 5:11.**

BARNABAS
SAW HIDDEN POTENTIAL.

W e all have times where we question our own worth or feel discouraged.

In those times, we need someone who believes in us, who sees our hidden potential, and speaks words of encouragement into our lives. Having someone who believes in us doesn't just make us feel better—it inspires us to act and move in a positive direction.

Barnabas shows us how to see people as God sees them. Deeper than a passing compliment or a friendly smile, encouragement requires a tenacious love, a persistent optimism, and a steadfast faith. Barnabas knew that to be an encourager involves sacrifice.

READ *IN THE GAP*, CHAPTER 5.

OPEN WITH PRAYER.

SHARE YOUR STORY

Would you describe yourself as a "glass half-full" person or a "glass half-empty" one? Why?

Today we are talking about Barnabas, whose name means "son of encouragement." He stood in the gap and befriended Saul when others didn't trust that he had really changed. Who is someone who encouraged you when you really needed it? How did they encourage you?

Capture any key thoughts, questions, and things you want to remember.

_____

_____

_____

_____

_____

_____

_____

_____

_____

DISCUSS THE FOLLOWING

Which of the individuals' testimonies was most meaningful to you? What made it stand out to you?

In the video, we met a woman who lost her sister when they were children. Her grandmother loved her and gave her attention and affirmation. Think of a child in your life—your own child, a niece or nephew, even a friend's child. What is one thing you can do to affirm and encourage that child?

As a biblical example, Barnabas wasn't looking for an easy life. He trusted God to give him eyes to see into the heart of a murderer and impart life and hope.

WILFREDO
DE JESÚS

IN
THE
GAP

WHAT HAPPENS WHEN
GOD'S PEOPLE STAND STRONG

Capture any key thoughts, questions,
and things you want to remember.

DISCUSS THE FOLLOWING

Pastor Choco shared how much Barnabas risked to befriend Saul.
What do we risk when we choose to encourage someone?

READ ACTS 9:19–31

Because Saul (before his encounter with Jesus) had been killing believers, many followers of Jesus didn't trust him. How did Barnabas stand in the gap for Saul?

Barnabas saw Saul's potential and encouraged and protected him. What result did Barnabas's faith in God and in Saul have?

READ ACTS 11:19–30; 12:25; AND CHAPTER 13

As time passed, their friendship resulted in effective ministry. How did God use these two men?

How does having someone stand in the gap for you and encourage you help you to do the same for others?

CHANGE YOUR STORY

GOD WANTS US TO BE PART OF HIS KINGDOM—TO WEAVE OUR STORY INTO HIS. THE HOLY SPIRIT HELPS US TO IDENTIFY THE GAPS IN OTHERS' LIVES AND THEN GIVES US THE STRENGTH TO STAND IN THOSE GAPS.

Barnabas saw hidden potential in others. He didn't wait for Saul to come to him. He left the comfort of a growing ministry to find one person, one man who would take the gospel to the farthest reaches of his world. Tell about a time someone stood in the gap for another person and God did something amazing as a result.

PERSONAL
REFLECTION

In the video, Pastor Choco said, "We all need encouragers." We all need someone in our lives who can speak into us, regardless of what we're going through. There's always an encouraging word that you can give somebody, and then watch the transformation that can happen. What keeps you from standing in the gap for others?

In his book, Pastor Choco asks challenging questions about how far we will go to stand in the gap. Prayerfully consider your answers to the following:

- Will you look past a person's accent or language to befriend someone from a different culture?

- Will you care so much about another person's tragic circumstances that you don't care what others think of you as you reach out?

- Will you sacrifice comfort for those in need?

- Will you set aside your agenda to get on God's agenda to love "the least of these"?

PRAYING
TOGETHER

How can the group pray together for you? (Add others' prayer requests here.)

CLOSE IN PRAYER.

DAILY
DEVOTIONS

"THEREFORE ENCOURAGE ONE ANOTHER AND BUILD EACH
OTHER UP, JUST AS IN FACT YOU ARE DOING"
1 THESSALONIANS 5:11.

*Developing our ability to follow the leading of the Holy Spirit takes
time and persistence. Learning how to stand in gap comes to us
day-by-day as we:*

PRAY. Commit to personal prayer and daily connection with God.
(You may find it helpful to write your prayers in a journal.)
Remember to pray for the requests shared by your fellow group
members.

MEMORIZE. Reflect on what God is saying about standing in the gap
for others by learning a passage of Scripture like the Theme Verse
above.

DAILY DEVOTIONS. Complete the Daily Devotions section. Each day, you'll
read just one portion of a passage of Scripture. Give prayerful
consideration to what God is telling you. Take your time! Ponder
and reflect. Then record your thoughts, insights, or prayer in the
Reflect section below the verses you read. On the sixth day, record
a summary of what you have learned about standing in the gap
through this study.

DAILY DEVOTIONS

Day 1.

1 THESSALONIANS 5:12

"Now we ask you, brothers and sisters, to acknowledge those who work hard among you, who care for you in the Lord and who admonish you."

REFLECT:

People who "admonish you" are those who both encourage and correct you. Do you have people like this in your life? If not, pray about whom you could invite into this sort of spiritual relationship.

Day 2.

1 THESSALONIANS 5:13

"Hold them in the highest regard in love because of their work. Live in peace with each other."

REFLECT:

Who is someone who needs to hear the words, "I hold you in the highest regard"? How would this encourage them?

Day 3.

1 THESSALONIANS 5:14

"And we urge you, brothers and sisters, warn those who are idle and disruptive, encourage the disheartened, help the weak, be patient with everyone."

REFLECT:

Who is someone who is disheartened? (Perhaps it is someone that no one else really wants to befriend.) How can you encourage that person, and be patient with them?

Day 4.

1 THESSALONIANS 5:16

"Make sure that nobody pays back wrong for wrong, but always strive to do what is good for each other and for everyone else."

REFLECT:

How would striving to do what is good for others be a way of encouraging them without ever saying a word? What specific ways can you do good for others?

Day 5.

1 THESSALONIANS 5:16–18

"Rejoice always, pray continually, give thanks in all circumstances; for this is God's will for you in Christ Jesus."

REFLECT:

How will doing the things listed in these verses help you to encourage others and to encourage yourself in your faith?

Day 6.

SUMMARY

Use the following space to write any thoughts God has put in your heart and mind about standing in the gap for others.

TAKING ACTION

How will you put these insights into action?

SESSION SIX

THEME VERSE: "When the angel of the Lᴏʀᴅ appeared to Gideon, he said, 'The Lᴏʀᴅ is with you, mighty warrior'" **Judges 6:12.**

GIDEON

WAS SENSITIVE TO THE VOICE OF GOD.

f ever there was an unlikely hero, it was Gideon. Hiding in a winepress, he is visited by an angel who calls him a mighty warrior. Gideon's immediate responses show he is anything but mighty. He argues with the angel, telling the angel that the battle plan will never work, and wonders why he, of all people, was chosen for this assignment.

God could have just wiped out the Midianites. Instead, God calls Gideon to stand in the gap and obey Him. Like Gideon, how we see ourselves— our low confidence, our feelings of inadequacy—these don't matter in God's eyes. He uses the weak to shame

READ *IN THE GAP*, CHAPTER 7.*

the strong, and He can turn anyone into a mighty warrior.

How much time do you spend arguing with God when He calls you to do something you think is beyond your capabilities? Wouldn't it make more sense to put our energy into finding out exactly what God is calling us to do, rather than trying to argue with Him about it?

OPEN WITH PRAYER.

*Not all book chapters are part of this study.

We build **COMMUNITY** and **CONNECTION** BY SHARING

OUR STORIES, OUR EXPERIENCES **of GOD.**

SHARE YOUR STORY

Have you ever had to be braver than you thought you could?
Tell the group about that time. What happened?

What keeps us from believing in ourselves and our abilities?

WILFREDO
DE JESUS

IN
THE
GAP

WHAT HAPPENS WHEN
GOD'S PEOPLE STAND STRONG

Capture any key thoughts, questions,
and things you want to remember.

_____

_____

_____

_____

_____

_____

_____

_____

_____

DISCUSS THE FOLLOWING

How did others hear from God to stand in the gap for the people
in the video?

One woman rejected others' love due to abuse in her past. How
can we persist and reach out to people who need to feel God's
love?

How can we stand in the gap for members of our family?

HEAR GOD'S STORY

HOW CAN WE BECOME A PART OF GOD'S STORY? BY ALIGNING OUR STORIES WITH HIS.

AS A BIBLICAL EXAMPLE, GIDEON REMINDS US THAT GOD SOMETIMES MAKES COWARDS INTO HEROES.

Capture any key thoughts, questions,
and things you want to remember.

DISCUSS THE FOLLOWING

Pastor Choco shares that Gideon had a low self-esteem and then encounters an angel that calls him a "mighty warrior." God feels that way about us too. What makes it difficult for us to believe that?

READ JUDGES 6:11–16

As you read this story, how would you describe Gideon?

What does Gideon accuse God of?

What does Gideon say about himself? Why do you think he has such low self-esteem?

What does God promise Gideon?

Gideon came out of his hiding place and began to do the work of the Lord. What hiding place might God be calling you out of? What work is He calling you to do?

CHANGE YOUR STORY

GOD WANTS US TO BE PART OF HIS KINGDOM—TO WEAVE OUR STORY INTO HIS. THE HOLY SPIRIT HELPS US TO IDENTIFY THE GAPS IN OTHERS' LIVES AND THEN GIVES US THE STRENGTH TO STAND IN THOSE GAPS.

It took a while for Gideon to believe that God could really make him a mighty warrior. In his book, Pastor Choco reminds us that our own self-talk—especially after we have experienced failure or rejection—speaks volumes about what we really believe about God and ourself. How does Gideon's story demonstrate this?

How have you seen someone else struggle with negative self-talk? What might a person do to overcome that limitation?

PERSONAL
REFLECTION

In the video, we heard, "God looks not at our present situation; He looks at our future or what our destiny is to be." What does God see when He looks at you?

In his book, Pastor Choco reminds us, "Don't let the wounds and fears of the past dictate your present and your future. Hear God's voice. Be strong and brave. He is still speaking. Are you listening, mighty warrior?" Pause now and listen for God's voice. Ask Him to help you see yourself as His warrior.

PRAYING
TOGETHER

Share with your group how God has changed your story during this study. How will you stand in the gap?

What battle are you facing that you have no way of winning unless God helps you? How can the group pray together for you? (Add others' prayer requests here.)

CLOSE IN PRAYER.

DAILY
DEVOTIONS

"WHEN THE ANGEL OF THE LORD APPEARED TO GIDEON, HE SAID, 'THE LORD IS WITH YOU, MIGHTY WARRIOR'"
JUDGES 6:12.

Developing our ability to follow the leading of the Holy Spirit takes time and persistence. Learning how to stand in gap comes to us day-by-day as we:

PRAY. Commit to personal prayer and daily connection with God. (You may find it helpful to write your prayers in a journal.) Remember to pray for the requests shared by your fellow group members.

MEMORIZE. Reflect on what God is saying about standing in the gap for others by learning a passage of Scripture like the Theme Verse above.

DAILY DEVOTIONS. Complete the Daily Devotions section. Each day, you'll read just one portion of a passage of Scripture. Give prayerful consideration to what God is telling you. Take your time! Ponder and reflect. Then record your thoughts, insights, or prayer in the Reflect section below the verses you read. On the sixth day, record a summary of what you have learned about standing in the gap through this study.

DAILY
DEVOTIONS

Day 1.

PSALM 44:4
"You are my King and my God, who decrees victories for Jacob."

REFLECT:
What victories do you need God to give you? Where are you struggling to trust that He'll come through for you?

Day 2.

PSALM 44:5
"Through you we push back our enemies; through your name we trample our foes."

REFLECT:
What foes and enemies do you face right now (they may be intangible things like fear, doubt, insecurity)? What does God promise in this verse?

Day 3.

PSALM 44:6
"I put no trust in my bow, my sword does not bring me victory."

REFLECT:
What does this verse say about our own efforts to fight the battles of life?

Day 4.

PSALM 44:7
"But you give us
victory over our
enemies, you put our
adversaries to shame."

REFLECT:
What does having God
beside us as we fight
the battles of life do for
us?

Day 5.

PSALM 44:8
"In God we make our
boast all day long, and
we will praise your name
forever."

REFLECT:
Spend some time just
praising God. Then, think
about this: How can you
boast about God today
when you speak to
other people?

Day 6.

SUMMARY
Use the following space
to write any thoughts
God has put in your
heart and mind about
standing in the gap for
others.

TAKING ACTION
How will you put these
insights into action?

EXTRA HELPS

LEADERSHIP
TRAINING 101

CONGRATULATIONS! YOU HAVE RESPONDED TO THE CALL TO HELP SHEPHERD JESUS' FLOCK. THERE ARE FEW OTHER TASKS IN THE FAMILY OF GOD THAT SURPASS THE CONTRIBUTION YOU WILL MAKE. AS YOU PREPARE TO LEAD, WHETHER IT IS ONE SESSION OR THE ENTIRE SERIES, HERE ARE A FEW THOUGHTS TO KEEP IN MIND. WE ENCOURAGE YOU TO READ THESE AND REVIEW THEM WITH EACH NEW DISCUSSION LEADER BEFORE THAT PERSON LEADS.

1 Remember that you are not alone. God knows everything about you, and He knew that you would be asked to lead your group. Remember that it is common for all good leaders to feel that they are not ready to lead. Moses, Solomon, Jeremiah, and Timothy—they all were reluctant to lead. God promises, "Never will I leave you; never will I forsake you" (Hebrews 13:5). Whether you are leading for one evening, for several weeks, or for a lifetime, you will be blessed as you serve.

2 Don't try to do it alone. Pray right now for God to help you build a healthy leadership team. If you can enlist a coleader to help you lead the group, you will find your experience to be much richer. This is your chance to involve as many people as you can in building a healthy group. All you have to do is call and ask people to help. You'll be surprised at the response.

3 Just be yourself. If you won't be you, who will? God wants to use your unique gifts and temperament. Don't try to do things exactly like another leader; do them in a way that fits you! Just admit it when you don't have an answer, and apologize when you make a mistake. Your group will love you for it, and you'll sleep better at night!

4 Prepare for your meeting ahead of time. Review the DVD session and the leader's notes in this guide, and write down your responses to each question. Pay special attention to exercises that ask group members to do something other than engage in discussion.

These exercises will help your group live what the Bible teaches, not just talk about it. Be sure you understand how an exercise works, and bring any necessary supplies (such as paper and pens) to your meeting. Finally review "Outline of Each Session" (page 6) so you'll remember the purpose of each section in the study.

5 Pray for your group members by name. Before you begin your session, go around the room in your mind and pray for each member by name. You may want to review the prayer list at least once a week. Ask God to use your time together to touch the heart of every person uniquely. Expect God to lead you to whomever He wants you to encourage or challenge in a special way. If you listen, God will surely lead!

6 When you ask a question, be patient. Someone will eventually respond. Sometimes people need a moment or two of silence to think about the question, and if silence doesn't bother you, it won't bother anyone else. After someone responds, affirm the response with a simple "thanks" or "good job." Then ask, "How about somebody else?" or "Would someone who hasn't shared like to add anything?" Be sensitive to new people or reluctant members who aren't ready to talk or pray in a group setting. If you give them a safe setting, they will blossom over time.

7 Provide transitions between questions. When guiding the discussion, always read aloud the transitional paragraphs and the questions. Ask the group if anyone would like to read the paragraph or Bible passage. Don't call on anyone, but ask for a volunteer, and then be patient until someone begins. Be sure to thank the person who reads aloud.

8 Break up into smaller groups each week, or people won't stay. If your group has more than seven people, we strongly encourage you to have the group gather sometimes in discussion circles of three or four people during the Sharing Together sections of the study. With a greater opportunity to talk in a small circle, people will connect more with the study, apply more quickly what they're learning, and ultimately get more out of it. A small circle also encourages a quiet person to participate and tends to minimize the effects of a more vocal or dominant member. It can also help people feel more loved in your group. When you gather again at the end of the section, you can have one person summarize the highlights from each circle.

Small circles are also helpful during prayer time. People who are unaccustomed to praying aloud will feel more comfortable trying it with just two or three others. Also, prayer requests won't take as much time, so circles will have more time to actually pray. When you gather back with the whole group, you can have one person from each circle briefly update everyone on the prayer requests. People are more willing to pray in small circles if they know that the whole group will hear all the prayer requests.

LEADING FOR
THE FIRST TIME

Sweaty palms are a healthy sign. The Bible says God is gracious to the humble. Remember who is in control; if you feel inadequate, that is probably a good sign. Those who are soft in heart (and sweaty palmed) are those whom God is sure to speak through.

Seek support. Ask your leader, coleader, or close friend to pray for you and prepare with you before the session. Walking through the study will help you anticipate potentially difficult questions and discussion topics.

Bring your uniqueness to the study. Lean into who you are and how God wants you to lead the study uniquely.

Prepare. Prepare. Prepare. Go through the session several times. If you are using the DVD, listen to the teaching segment and then choose the questions you want to be sure to discuss.

Ask for feedback so you can grow. Perhaps in an e-mail or on cards handed out at the study, have everyone write down three things you did well and one thing you could improve on. Don't get defensive, but show an openness to learn and grow.

Prayerfully consider launching a new group. This doesn't need to happen overnight, but God's heart is for this to happen over time. Not all Christians are called to be leaders or teachers, but we are all called to be "shepherds" of a few someday.

Share with your group what God is doing in your heart. God is searching for those whose hearts are fully His. Share your trials and victories. We promise that people will relate.

HOSTING
AN OPEN HOUSE

If you're starting a new group, try planning an open house before your first formal group meeting. Even if you have only two to four core members, it's a great way to break the ice and to consider prayerfully who else might be open to join you over the next few weeks. You can also use this kickoff meeting to hand out study guides, spend some time getting to know each other, discuss each person's expectations for the group, and briefly pray for each other.

A simple meal or good desserts always make a kickoff meeting more fun. After people introduce themselves and share how they ended up being at the meeting (you can play a game to see who has the wildest story!), have everyone respond to a few icebreaker questions: "What is your favorite family vacation?" or "What is one thing you love about your church/our community?" or "What are three things about your life growing up that most people here don't know?"

Next, ask everyone to tell what he or she hopes to get out of the study. You might want to review the Small Group Agreement (page 114) and talk about each person's expectations and priorities.

Finally, set an empty chair (maybe two) in the center of your group and explain that it represents someone who would enjoy or benefit from this group but who isn't here yet. Ask people to pray about whom they could invite to join the group over the next few weeks. Hand out postcards and have everyone write an invitation or two. Don't worry about ending up with too many people; you can always have one discussion circle in the living room and another in the dining room after you watch the session. Each group could then report prayer requests and progress at the end of the session.

You can skip this kickoff meeting if your time is limited, but you'll experience a huge benefit if you take the time to connect with each other in this way.

SMALL GROUP
FAQs

What do we do on the first night of our group?

Like all fun things in life—have a party! A "get to know you" coffee, dinner, or dessert night is a great way to launch a new study. You may want to review the Small Group Agreement (page 94) and share the names of a few friends you can invite to join you. But most importantly, have fun before your study time begins.

Where do we find new members for our group?

We encourage you to pray with your group and then brainstorm a list of people from work, church, your neighborhood, your children's school, family, the gym, and so forth. Then have each group member invite several of the people on his or her list.

No matter how you find participants, it's vital that you stay on the lookout for new people to join your group. All groups tend to go through healthy attrition—the result of moves, releasing new leaders, ministry opportunities, and so forth—and if the group gets too small, it could be at risk of shutting down. If you and your group stay open, you'll be amazed at the people God sends your way. The next person just might become a friend for life. You never know!

How long will this group meet?

It's totally up to the group once you come to the end of this six-week study. Most groups meet weekly for at least their first six weeks, but every other week can work as well.

At the end of this study, each group member may decide if he or she wants to continue on for another six-week study. Some groups launch relationships for years to come, and others are stepping-stones into another group experience. Either way, enjoy the journey.

What if this group is not working for us?

You're not alone! This could be the result of a personality conflict, life stage difference, geographical distance, level of spiritual maturity, or any number of things. Relax. Pray for God's direction, and at the end of this six-week study, decide whether to continue with this group or find another. You don't buy the first car you look at or marry the first person you date, and the same goes with a group. Don't bail out before the six weeks are up—God might have something to teach you. Also, don't run from conflict or prejudge people before you have given them a chance. God is still working in you too!

How do we handle the child care needs in our group?

We suggest that you empower the group to openly brainstorm solutions. You may try one option that works for a while and then adjust over time. Our favorite approach is for adults to meet in the living room or dining room and to share the cost of a babysitter (or two) who can be with the kids in a different part of the house. In this way, parents don't have to be away from their children all evening when their children are too young to be left at home. A second option is to use one home for the kids and a second home (close by or a phone call away) for the adults. A third idea is to rotate the responsibility of providing a lesson or care for the children either in the same home or in another home nearby. This can be an incredible blessing for kids. Finally, the most common idea is to decide that you need to have a night to invest in your spiritual life individually or as a couple and to make your own arrangements for child care. No matter what decision the group makes, the best approach is to dialogue openly about both the problem and the solution.

SMALL GROUP
AGREEMENT

Our Expectations:
To provide a predictable environment where participants experience authentic community and spiritual growth

Group Attendance	To give priority to the group meeting. We will call or e-mail if we will be late or absent. (Completing the Group Calendar will minimize this issue.)
Safe Environment	To help create a safe place where people can be heard and feel loved. (Please, no quick answers, snap judgments, or simple fixes.)
Respect Differences	To be gentle and gracious to people with different spiritual maturity, personal opinions, temperaments, or "imperfections" in fellow group members. We are all works in progress.
Confidentiality	To keep anything that is shared strictly confidential and within the group, and to avoid sharing improper information about those outside the group.
Encouragement for Growth	To be not just takers but givers of life. We want to spiritually multiply our life by serving others with our God-given gifts.
Shared Ownership	To remember that every member is a minister and to ensure that each attender will share a small team role or responsibility over time.
Rotating Hosts/ Leaders and Homes	To encourage different people to host the group in their homes, and to rotate the responsibility of facilitating each meeting. (See the Small Group Calendar.)

Our Times Together:
- Refreshments _____
- Child care _____
- When we will meet (day of week) _____
- Where we will meet (place) _____
- We will begin at (time) _____ and end at _____
- We will do our best to have some or all of us attend a worship service together.

  Our primary worship service time will be _____
- Date of this agreement _____
- Date we will review this agreement again _____
- Who (other than the leader) will review this agreement at the end of this study

  _____

MEETING
STRUCTURE

Small groups gather not just to answer questions or to study a text, but to deepen their connection with God and with one another. We suggest that every meeting include not just study, but times of sharing, worship, and prayer. Every week, include the following elements:

SHARING

At your first or second meeting, use the Circles of Life diagram on the next page to write the names of two or three people you know who need to know Christ. Commit to pray for God's guidance and an opportunity to share with each of them. At subsequent meetings, check how group members are doing at reaching out to the people they've each listed on their circles chart.

PRAYER

Allow everyone to answer this question: "How can we pray for you this week?" Be sure to write prayer requests in each session's prayer segment.

WORSHIP

Spend a few minutes worshipping God together. Here are two ideas:

- Have someone use their musical gifts to lead the group in a worship song. Try singing a cappella, using a worship CD, or have someone accompany your singing with a musical instrument.

- Read a passage of Scripture together, making it a time of praise and worship as the words remind you of all God has done for you. Choose a psalm or other favorite verse.

CIRCLES
OF LIFE

Family

(immediate or extended)

_____

_____

_____

Familiar

(neighbors, kids' sports teams,
school, etc.)

_____

_____

_____

Friends

_____

_____

_____

Fun

(gym, hobbies, hangouts)

_____

_____

_____

Firm

(work)

_____

_____

_____

ABOUT THE AUTHOR

Widely known as "Pastor Choco," Wilfredo De Jesús is the Senior Pastor of New Life Covenant Church in Chicago. Under Pastor Choco's leadership, New Life Covenant is the largest church in the Assemblies of God fellowship.

Wilfredo was born and raised in Chicago's Humboldt Park community. When he was seventeen years old, he received Jesus as his Lord and Savior at a small Pentecostal Spanish-speaking church in the community. From that moment, his life was forever transformed.

He remained in that same little church for over twenty years before he was appointed Senior Pastor in July 2000. Since then, the church has grown from a weekly attendance of 120 to 17,000 globally through church plants and more than 130 ministries reaching the most disenfranchised—the brokenhearted, poor, homeless, prostitutes, drug addicts, and gang members.

Rev. De Jesús has been instrumental in the development of several community-based programs such as New Life Family Services, which operates a homeless shelter for women with children. Some of the church's other vital ministries include the Chicago Master's Commission, an intensive discipleship program for college-age students, and the Chicago Dream Center, which offers various programs and services to assist individuals and families to move toward self-sufficiency and to overcome poverty and its ill effects.

Pastor Choco's vision is simple: to be a church for the hurting that reaches people for Jesus.

In 2012, Wilfredo released his first book, *Amazing Faith*, in which he shares his life story and message: "No one is beyond the transforming power of God's love. When we let Him, God

fills our hearts with His love, strength, and purpose, and we become complete."

In April 2013, De Jesús was named one of TIME Magazine's 100 most influential people in the world and recognized for his leadership and influence with the Evangelical and Latino audiences. He wants others to understand that his accomplishments are based on a life dedicated to God and His purposes. In other words, whatever the accomplishment, to God be the glory!

De Jesús is sought after as a motivational speaker at various church events, leadership conferences, and assemblies throughout the nation and abroad. He resides in the Humboldt Park community of Chicago with his wife Elizabeth. They have three children, Alexandria, Yesenia, and Wilfredo, Jr., and a son-in-law, Anthony Gomez.

f pastorwilfredodejesus

y PastorChoco

OTHER RESOURCES BY WILFREDO DE JESÚS

In the Gap book (English) 978-1-93830-989-2
In the Gap ePDF (English) 978-1-93830-990-8
In the Gap epub (English) 978-1-93830-991-5
In the Gap small-group DVD (English)
    978-1-62912-099-7
In the Gap study guide (English) 978-1-62912-097-3

In the Gap book (Spanish) 978-1-93830-992-2
In the Gap ePDF (Spanish) 978-1-93830-993-9
In the Gap epub (Spanish) 978-1-93830-994-6
In the Gap small-group DVD (Spanish)
    978-1-62912-100-0
In the Gap study guide (Spanish) 978-1-62912-098-0

Amazing Faith book (English) 978-1-93669-995-7
Amazing Faith ePDF (English) 978-1-93669-996-4
Amazing Faith epub (English) 978-1-93669-997-1

Amazing Faith book (Spanish) 978-1-93783-058-8
Amazing Faith ePDF (Spanish) 978-1-93783-059-5
Amazing Faith epub (Spanish) 978-1-93783-060-1

For more information about these resources visit
www.influenceresources.com